Good Mor[ning]
Little Pretty Girl

A Life Journal and Adult Coloring Book

WRITTEN BY TABITHA HALL-PENNON
ILLUSTRATED BY VANESSA J. THOMPSON

I would like to dedicate this book to:

My Dad, Terry Lee Hall
My Grandmother, Annie Mae Griffin
My Aunt, Berline Hall-McBride
and to My Bus Driver, Mr. Nolen

"Bye... Love You... Be Careful"
Thank you, Madison Massey, for these words!

T.H.P.

To book Mrs. Hall-Pennon for speaking engagements, please call:
469 684 9000

Tyler Street Place #200
610 E. Tyler Street
Ennis, Texas 75119

Adult Coloring Page Illustrations drawn by Vanessa J. Thompson. See more samples of her work and contact her on her web site: [www (dot) vanessajthompson (dot) com].

ISBN: 978-0-359-91651-1

Who Is This Good Morning Little Pretty Girl...?

I am Tabitha Hall-Pennon.

I am a wife of a wonderful guy and a mother of two awesome children, Teri and Willie. I am a Certified Mindfulness Movement Teacher. I am a Life Coach. I am a Doula and an Author.

I grew up on Tyler Street in Ennis, Texas, graduated from Ennis High School, attended Tyler Junior College in Tyler, Texas, Texas Southern University in Houston, Texas and graduated from Eastfield College with a dual degree in Substance Abuse and Social Work.

I enjoy camping and spending time in my Vintage Camper (Journey), adult coloring, and spending time with my family. I am a woman that enjoys wearing many hats, I LIVE! I do not want to leave this earth with any regrets. As you will learn about me through the pages, you will see I am definitely a risk taker. I have been that way all my life and the older I get, the more I take risks, only now they are healthier and safer risks.

I now sit the intentions to introduce you to healing through *Good Morning, Little Pretty Girl*, as I have.
Good Morning, Little Pretty Girl is my story. A story that I am sure many can relate to. I invite you to enter into my world, while coloring and journaling. Come with me.

All you need is to bring Your Truth and Your Open Mind!

This Little Girl

This little girl was raised by her father, grandmother and aunt, growing up with her cousins that were more like sisters. She grew up with people that she felt loved her. This little girl grew up in a lie! She later found out the people, who raised her, who she thought to be her family, who she loved and still love wasn't her blood family, he wasn't her father.

That little girl is ME!

I felt loved and accepted, but there were times I felt disconnected. As I got older, I was told from others who my father really was, even when asked. I was offended because I knew that couldn't be true. In high school, I was often asked if I was the sister of a young lady who was very popular and super smart. Not only was she popular and smart, she was beautiful. I couldn't figure out why people thought that. I was told, "You look just like her!" I even sometimes thought to myself… "I wish!"

As an adult, I still struggle with the one person that should have been honest with me. However, she still chooses to live in denial.

How can you relate to growing up in a lie?

_____

_____

_____

Have you been a part of not being honest with someone you love?

_____

_____

_____

_____

The Bus Driver

Mr. Nolen was a school bus driver, whom was also an important driver of my future!

When I was a little girl, I stood at the bus stop waiting with my two ponytails held by rubber bands from the Ennis Daily Newspaper styled by my grandmother, whom combed my hair the best she could. I've always desired getting "turls," my word for "curls," like the other girls from school. I was always told "no," leaving me feeling ugly and embarrassed. I felt alone and empty, but loved. Then, things got better.

Getting on to the bus, Mr. Nolen would greet me and say, "Good morning, little pretty girl!" And for that moment, that bus ride to Travis Elementary, I felt like I was a little pretty girl. My cousin told me, "He probably says that to all the little girls..." And perhaps he did. But for me, it resonated in my heart and mind; it got into my soul. From Mondays to Fridays, for fifteen minutes, I believed him. The more Mr. Nolen said it, the more I believed it!

He planted the seed!

Who would you identify as your "bus driver", the person, place, or thing that planted a seed for you? Was it a good or bad seed?

_____

_____

_____

_____

_____

_____

_____

The First of My "A" Words
ABANDONMENT

My parents divorced when I was very young. When they divorced, my mother took my two brothers and moved into her own place. My dad and I moved in with my grandmother, his mother. Being young I never questioned why she took my brothers and not me. After all I was happy to be with my dad, grandmother and aunt, for years I even thought my aunt was my mother, we have a very strong bond, had it then and still today.

Of course the older I got I figured out that she was my aunt and not my mother. Still I continued to go with the flow, I was with my family and that was what mattered. After discovering that I started to wonder why she left me? She took my brothers but not me.

Again I was loved so it didn't matter, I thought.

It wasn't until I working as a counselor and a colleague interviewed me for an assignment. She asked about my childhood and my relationship with my mother specifically. When I shared it, she said, "Back then, it was very unusual in the black family for the mother NOT to take all children, especially her daughter." That hit me like a ton of bricks! I began to cry and said to myself... "Why did she not want me?"

This little girl was finally wanting to know the answer to that question.

Have you ever felt a sense of abandonment?

_____

_____

What things or aspects in your life have you abandoned?

_____

_____

How did it make you feel and why?

_____

_____

_____

9

My Second "A" Word
ANGER

I grew up surrounded by love, however, there was so much anger. Anger that lived inside me and I questioned why I felt anger. My anger was within, I wouldn't dare express it to my family, so I held it inside of my soul. I would get angry but I didn't know why I was angry. Now as an adult, I can actually see I was depressed.

I remember fighting in school, mainly males, again not sure why, but I would target the boys to explode on. While at the age of about 8 or 9 until about 15, I didn't see my actions as SO bad, I knew there was an issue. Fighting, crying and one point I remember being suicidal.

My childhood issues were definitely issues, it even came to haunt me as an adult. While working on this book, I was approached by a classmate. She shared with me the negative impact I had on her life, that I bullied her throughout school, some 40 years later she still carried some resentment towards me. I have to be honest, I didn't remember but I didn't deny it because I know what I may have been capable of. I apologized to her and invited her to do as I have done...Start YOUR healing.

Have you been angry, if so why?

_____

_____

_____

Are you in YOUR healing process, if so what does that look like?

_____

_____

_____

_____

_____

The Last "A" Word
ABORTION

This word has many meanings. For ME, it meant ending a pregnancy at the age of 14.

Attending the school dance on Saturday and preparing to have an abortion on Monday. It was done. I stood there in so much emotional pain, fear and shame; not sure where my soul would go when I die. Growing up in church, abortions were always thought to be murder. It was only defined as that!

My decision to have an abortion was not talked about. I was not blaming the church or anyone else for my actions or decisions. Some Christians today still tend to judge people who had abortion(s) and or wanting/needing to have one.
The abortion was totally my decision. He was totally against it. In fact, he wanted to tell his mother and talk to her before I had it done. NO WAY!

He shared with me that if I aborted the baby, that he would never have the opportunity to have children again. Until this day, I don't think he does.

What are your thoughts on aborting something?

_____

_____

_____

_____

What have you aborted in your life?

_____

_____

_____

Any regrets?

_____

_____

In My Valley

This season in my life, could not be drawn and colored, if there was a picture of DEATH and DANGEROUS Living, that's what the illustration would look like.

Early as my senior year in high school, I was looking for affection, looking for it through married men at the time. Now I said affection, not love, I never wanted to be in a relationship if there was love.

I had NO intentions of committing to anyone. Not sure why but I felt comfortable with knowing they would go back to the person they really loved. I apparently didn't love myself so I understood them not loving me... It was okay with me. I truly believe those women who prefer married men struggle with low or no self esteem. We, at some point, feel like we didn't deserve anything better. This was my truth!

My senior year in high school I was confronted by his wife, with a pistol pointed in my face. She assured me she would kill me about her husband, and yes, I believed her! They moved and I never heard from either one until years later. I was at a business meeting and she was there. She approached me and said, "You remember me?" I wasn't for sure at the time. I wasn't focusing on her face the last time I saw her, she immediately refreshed my memory. She told me who she was and WHOSE she was.

She also shared that they were no longer married.
That was a weird feeling...
Of course, at that time I had found myself. I was happily married with two children.

Another near death experience by another wife was with my affair with the truck driver. He was a very nice man, married for multiple years and one young daughter that was always accustomed to him bringing her things when he came home. While he would do his father/husband duties I would be in the mall or the hotel room, waiting on him.

One particular day he decided to just stop by their house, just in and out. He suggested that I stay in the sleeping area of the 18 wheeler. Not long after he went in, his daughter continues her route by coming to the truck to get her goodies...Well I'm usually not in there with her goodies. He realized it and stopped her from getting in the truck. That concerned his wife and she wanted answers as to why not this time! She proceeded to go in the house and I guess he knew his wife pretty well. He knew what she was going to get.

We took off and she followed us for miles while firing her pistol at the truck. After many miles, she stopped following us and shooting.

Hours later we stopped. There were several bullet holes in the truck.

I will NEVER forget that lady's name!

I eventually found MYSELF and wanted more than that life.

I started seeing a guy that wasn't married.

I had known for years. "I" fell in love... He taught me to see my value and to not allow the past to keep me stuck.

Most of all, he taught me what I needed to know when I had a second chance at love.

My Life Changer

This baby changed my life!

I did not know that she would. Never thinking about the night I cheated on the person who taught me how to love myself and what it felt like to love someone would be the reason why. I was pregnant. I carried her for the 9 months, 280 days. The generational curse in my family had caught up with me!

Having a baby that wasn't by the person I claimed to be the father, this wasn't unusual in my family.

I really thought he was the father. I sure did want him to be. I learned that if you love someone, you respect them and be submissive to them and them only.

This was a life lesson in so many ways.
No regrets for having my life changer. She has helped me to live, love, and laugh.

Who was your life changer?

_____

_____

_____

_____

_____

_____

_____

_____

This Place

Trinity Insurance Company.

THIS Place took me out of my comfort zone. I had been out of it before but not as a single mother, still broken... Just me and my Life Changer, my daughter, facing life in the big city of Dallas. I applied for the job when she was only 2 weeks old. They called me for the interview. I went against someone dear to me and took the job!

"Still Open" she said... "It's too soon for you to leave your baby."
I did it...scared and open!

Catching a van with 14 white women, well-established white women, was totally unfamiliar to me. I was broken, open and totally out of my comfort zone.
This Place is where life introduced me to living, to believing in a family life, meeting healthy people and believing that I didn't have to stay stuck in my past.

What place has inspired you?

_____

_____

_____

_____

_____

_____

_____

_____

_____

She Knew All The Time

This lady loves me and will let everyone know it! The "Aunt," who raised me and treated me like she did her own daughters, my cousins.
They were more like my big sisters.

As a child and as an adult, I've been protected by her. She knew that her brother really wasn't my biological father and that I wasn't really her niece. Even my cousins knew. But my "Aunt" always made sure they never used it against me. Even though they knew the truth, they never said anything to me.

I finally learned the truth as an adult in my 40s when one of my cousins posted on social media that "my uncle wasn't your biological father." Even after hearing that from outsiders for years, that post was the most impactful.

My aunt protected me and until this day still does. I've witnessed times when she'd introduce me as her niece, "Terry's daughter." Their response was a look as if they knew that wasn't true...Trust me I knew the look. She would say, "SHE MINE!" And I would feel so proud to be Terry's daughter and her niece.

Who protected you?

_____

_____

_____

_____

_____

_____

_____

_____

A Second Chance At Love

After finding myself, I realized I could have a second chance at love.

In spite of being told that I would never find a man that would want to marry me due to my past and the past of the females on my maternal side. This was told to me by a maternal family member... But let me tell you….THIS IS NOT TRUE!

I was blessed with an awesome husband. This man took my broken pieces and helped me put them back together. I found MYSELF and MY SOULMATE, and God joined us together.

Have YOU ever been given a Second Chance at Love?

_____

_____

_____

_____

_____

_____

_____

_____

_____

_____

Vision House

This is a place to develop a positive vision. A vision that became a reality for the little 7 year-old girl inside of me. The vision was to house and help women that suffered from addiction of drugs and/or alcohol. This vision has always been in my soul. In June 1999, it became a reality. I remember putting some pictures on a poster board with rooms with a bed, dresser and a night stand, where women would live!
A VISION BOARD!

Before I knew it, I would one day host Vision Board groups as an adult. In 1999, moving out of our first home and preparing to open Vision House in our first home. It appeared to me after living in our home for about 2 years that it was framed just like my poster board in 1974.

From June 15, 1999 to June 16, 2014, Vision House served over 5000 women. And for that I am so grateful!

Do you have a Vision?

_____

_____

_____

Have you made your vision a reality?

_____

_____

_____

_____

_____

_____

What Is Meant To Be... WILL BE!

We have come this far by faith. I knew it was possible for other people. I just did not think I deserved it.

This is US, THE PENNON FAMILY. This represents happiness, joy, love, tears, prayers, TRUTH and some growing pains, too.

They are adults now. They know my truth and still chose to love me. They still choose to call me their mother. But most of all, they respect me.

He met me when I was broken and still chose to love me. He chose to make me his WIFE, not his BC, side piece, old lady, or roommate but...........MRS. PENNON.

Will YOU trust your process?

_____

_____

_____

_____

_____

_____

_____

_____

_____

_____

I Believe Whatever You Say... Because It's YOU!

"STAY AWAY from water or you will die, you will drown."
All my life my grandmother told me that.

I believed her, especially after going on a softball trip to the pool with my teammates. I assumed that they weren't taught what I had been taught because they immediately got in the pool and started swimming.

I decided to join in. I was only getting into the pool where I could stand but then it dropped off into the deeper water. I was going to the bottom, fighting for my life until someone noticed me and pulled me out by my hair. They begin to pump my stomach to remove the water. All I could think about was that I was being punished by God for being disobedient to my grandmother that I loved so dearly. I never wanted to disappoint her. After all, she chose me. After that day, I said "Never again."
I believed that I would die next time just as she said.

At the age of 46, I decided that I would free myself from all the lies I was told. I took swimming lessons. I love swimming and being in the water. I haven't died yet!

Have you ever been told something by someone you love and trust to find out it was not true?

_____

_____

How do you forgive them and move forward?

_____

_____

_____

_____

_____

Journey is Her Name

Journey, my camper, is my safe space.

A space where I can not only take on a camping trip but where I can escape and just be me. Journey is where I can invite like-minded individuals with positive energy and intentions to share space with me.

I laugh, cry, mediate, pray, color, and journal in my camper, this is where I connect with my soul.

Where is YOUR Safe Space... Who do you invite into your safe space?

_____

_____

_____

_____

_____

_____

_____

_____

_____

From *Good Morning, Little Pretty Girl,*
the Caterpillar to...

Good Morning, Little Pretty Girl,
the Butterfly!